The Sea Otters of California

by Jane Duden

Content Consultant:
Ellen Faurot-Daniels
Science Director
Friends of the Sea Otter

Hilltop Books

An Imprint of Franklin Watts
A Division of Grolier Publishing
New York London Hong Kong Sydney
Danbury, Connecticut

Hilltop Books
http://publishing.grolier.com
Copyright © 1998 by Capstone Press • All rights reserved
Published simultaneously in Canada • Printed in the United States of America

Library of Congress Cataloging-in-Publication Data
Duden, Jane.
    The sea otters of California / by Jane Duden.
      p. cm. -- (Animals of the world)
    Includes bibliographical references (p. 23) and index.
    Summary: Introduces the world of sea otters, their physical
characteristics, behavior, and interaction with humans.
    ISBN 1-56065-578-X
    1. Sea otter--California--Juvenile literature. [1. Sea otter.
2. Otters.] I. Title. II. Series.
QL737.C25D84 1998
599.769′5′09794--dc21   97-11368
                                             CIP
                                             AC

Photo credits
Bob Cranston, cover, 4, 6, 8, 10, 12, 14, 16, 18, 20

Table of Contents

About Sea Otters

California sea otters are mammals that live in water. A mammal is a warm-blooded animal that has a backbone. Warm-blooded means that an animal's body is always the same temperature. Temperature is how hot or cold something is. Baby mammals drink milk from their mothers' bodies.

California sea otters are carnivores. A carnivore is an animal that eats meat. Sea otters eat many kinds of sea animals, especially shellfish. Shellfish include crabs, mussels, and clams.

Male sea otters weigh 65 pounds (29 kilograms) on average. They are about four and one half feet (one and one half meters) long. This measure includes the tail. Female sea otters are a little smaller. They weigh an average of 45 pounds (20 kilograms). Female sea otters are about four feet (about one meter) long.

California sea otters are mammals that live in water.

What Sea Otters Look Like

Sea otters have long bodies with wide, flat tails. Thick, dark brown fur covers their bodies. Sea otters have thicker fur than any other mammal. It helps keep them warm in the cold water.

Sea otters have dark eyes and small ears. Their ears close when they swim underwater. Long whiskers grow near their small noses. These whiskers help sea otters find food. Whiskers help them feel the water moving when an animal swims nearby.

Sea otters have two front paws with claws. They clean their fur with their front paws. They also use them to grab and eat food.

Sea otters' large back feet have long, webbed toes. Webbed means having skin between the toes. Sea otters use their back feet to swim.

Sea otters' legs have thin fur. Otters hold their legs out of the water while floating on their backs. This keeps their feet warm and dry.

Sea otters hold their legs out of the water.

Where Sea Otters Live

California sea otters live along the coast of central California in the Pacific Ocean. Some live on San Nicolas Island. They live where the water is not too deep. The water they live in is 50 to 75 feet (15 to 23 meters) deep.

Sea otters make their homes in kelp forests. Kelp is a kind of seaweed. It grows from the bottom of the ocean. Sea otters often wrap themselves in kelp while resting. This keeps them from floating away. California sea otters rarely leave the water. They may climb onto land if they are cold or scared.

Each sea otter has a home area called its range. Sea otters do not usually mind other sea otters swimming in their range. Sea otters often rest and play in groups called rafts. A raft may include any number of sea otters, from two to 200. Males often raft with other males. Females raft with other females and pups. Sometimes one male rafts with several females and their pups.

Sea otters wrap themselves in kelp while resting.

What Sea Otters Do

Sea otters spend about six hours a day eating. They must eat a lot of food to stay warm. They can eat 10 to 15 pounds (about five to seven kilograms) of food every day.

Sea otters dive to the ocean floor to find food. They stay underwater for 50 to 90 seconds. Then they bring the food up to the surface.

Sea otters float on their backs while eating. They hold their food on their chests. Sea otters mostly eat shellfish. They need to break the shells open. They use rocks as tools to break the shells. Sea otters are among the few mammals that use tools.

Sea otters spend a lot of time grooming their fur. Groom means to clean. Sea otters pull out dirt with their tongue and front paws. They roll in the water to rinse out the dirt. Then they blow air into their fur. The layers of air and fur keep sea otters warm.

Sea otters use rocks to crack open shellfish.

Sea Otter Enemies and Dangers

Sea otters have only a few natural predators. A predator is an animal that hunts other animals for food. White sharks and killer whales have been known to hunt sea otters. Bald eagles sometimes hunt young sea otters.

People are the greatest danger to sea otters. One big problem is oil spills. Ships carrying oil sometimes have accidents. They can spill oil into the ocean. Oil covers sea otters and makes their fur stick together. Cold water soaks their skin. Many sea otters have frozen to death after oil spills. They also swallow oil when they lick their fur. This makes sea otters sick.

Fishing nets are another danger. Sea otters sometimes become trapped in nets. They cannot swim to the surface to breathe air. This causes the sea otters to drown.

These sea otters are recovering from an oil spill.

Mating and Reproduction

Male and female sea otters usually live apart. They spend time together only to mate. Mate means to join together to produce young.

Sea otters can mate at any time during the year. Females are ready to mate when they are four years old. Males are ready when they are six years old.

To mate, a male swims up to a raft of females. He looks for a female that is ready to mate. If a female is not ready, she pushes him away. She lets him come closer if she wants to mate.

The female and the male swim and play. They stay together for three or four days. After mating, the female swims away from the male.

Female sea otters give birth four to six months after mating. California sea otters usually give birth in the water.

During mating, male and female otters swim and play together.

Newborn and Young Sea Otters

Newborn sea otters are called pups. A sea otter pup weighs three to five pounds (about one to two kilograms) at birth. Its long fur is light brown or yellow.

The female sea otter carries her pup on her chest. She keeps it safe and warm. She feeds the pup milk from her body. She grooms its fur several times a day. She wraps it in kelp when she dives for food. It floats until its mother returns.

A pup learns to swim when it is a few weeks old. It can eat solid food after one or two months. But it still drinks its mother's milk for six to eight months.

A female sea otter teaches her pup how to groom its fur. She also shows her pup how to find and eat food. A sea otter pup leaves its mother after six to eight months. It swims away to live on its own.

A female sea otter carries her pup on her chest.

Other Kinds of Otters

There are 12 kinds of otters. Most otters live on land and spend some time in lakes and rivers. Sea otters are the only otters that always live in or near the ocean.

There are many kinds of river otters. Two are the Eurasian river otter and the North American river otter. River otters are smaller than sea otters. They also have shorter fur.

River otters rest and give birth to young on land. They move better on land than sea otters do. River otters find food in rivers and lakes. They use all four legs to swim. They eat mostly fish.

There is just one other kind of sea otter. It is called the Alaska sea otter. Alaska sea otters live on the coasts of islands in the northern Pacific Ocean. They are like California sea otters, but there are some differences. Alaska sea otters leave the water more often. They are bigger than California sea otters.

Alaska sea otters are bigger than California sea otters.

Sea Otters and People

People have been enemies of sea otters. People began hunting sea otters for their fur in the 1700s. Hunters sold sea otter fur for a high price. In the 1900s, people became concerned that so many sea otters were dying. Many countries agreed to stop hunting sea otters in 1911.

People worked to make safe places for sea otters. Over time, the number of sea otters has grown. About 2,000 California sea otters live in the Pacific Ocean today.

Many people still want to protect sea otters. After oil spills, people clean the oil from otters' fur. Some groups try to move sea otters away from places where oil spills happen.

People have also passed many laws to help sea otters. It is against the law to harm a sea otter near California. With the help of people, there will always be sea otters.

People have been enemies of sea otters.

Fast Facts

Common name: California sea otter; also known as southern sea otter

Scientific name: Enhydra lutris

Life span: up to 30 years in zoos

Length: Adult male sea otters are about four and one half feet (one and one half meters) long. Females are a little shorter.

Weight: Adult male sea otters weigh about 65 pounds (20 kilograms). Females weigh a little less.

Features: Sea otters have long bodies with thick fur. They have small ears that close underwater. Their back feet have long webbed toes.

Population: There are about 2,000 California sea otters.

Home: California sea otters live along the coast of central California in the Pacific Ocean.

Diet: California sea otters eat mostly shellfish, such as crabs, mussels, and clams.

Words to Know

kelp (KELP)—a tall kind of seaweed that grows from the ocean floor

mammal (MAM-uhl)—a warm-blooded animal that has a backbone

mate (MAIT)—to join together to produce young

oil spill (OYL SPIL)—accidental spill of oil from a ship

predator (PRED-uh-tur)—an animal that hunts other animals for food

pup (PUHP)—newborn sea otter

raft (RAFT)—a floating group of sea otters

webbed (WEBD)—having skin between the toes

Read More

Brust, Beth Wagner. *Zoobooks: Sea Otters.* San Diego: Wildlife Education, Ltd., 1990.

Graves, Jack A. *What is a California Sea Otter?* Pacific Grove, Calif: The Boxwood Press, 1977.

Kalman, Bobbie. *Sea Otters.* New York: Crabtree, 1997.

Useful Addresses

The Cousteau Society
870 Greenbrier Circle,
Suite 402
Chesapeake, VA 23320

Vancouver Public Aquarium
PO Box 3232
Vancouver, British Columbia
Canada V6B 3X8

Internet Sites

Friends of the Sea Otter
http://www.seaotters.org
Animal Bytes: Sea Otter
http://www.bev.net/education/SeaWorld/animal_bytes/
sea_otterab.html

Index